T0124708

YOUR
INVISIBLE
POWER

ORIGINAL CLASSIC EDITIONS

Atom-Smashing Power of Mind

Crystallizing Public Opinion

How to Attract Money

Narrative of the Life of Frederick Douglass

Self Mastery Through Conscious Autosuggestion

The Art of War

The Magic of Believing

The Master Key System

The Power of Your Subconscious Mind

The Prince

The Richest Man in Babylon

The Science of Getting Rich

The Secret of the Ages

Think and Grow Rich

Think Your Way to Wealth

Your Invisible Power

YOUR INVISIBLE POWER

Genevieve Behrend

MEDIA

Published 2021 by Gildan Media LLC
aka G&D Media
www.GandDmedia.com

YOUR INVISIBLE POWER. Copyright © 2021 by G&D Media. Copyright 1921, 1927 by Genevieve Behrend. Preface copyright © 2021 by Mitch Horowitz. All rights reserved.

No part of this book may be reproduced or transmitted in any form, by any means, (electronic, photocopying, recording, or otherwise) without the prior written permission of the author. No liability is assumed with respect to the use of the information contained within. Although every precaution has been taken, the author and publisher assume no liability for errors or omissions. Neither is any liability assumed for damages resulting from the use of the information contained herein.

Front cover design by David Rheinhardt of Pyrographx

Interior design by Meghan Day Healey of Story Horse, LLC

Library of Congress Cataloging-in-Publication Data is available upon request

ISBN: 978-1-7225-0275-1

10   9   8   7   6   5   4   3   2   1

CONTENTS

PREFACE
Your Miracle Hour
by Mitch Horowitz

Rediscovering *Your Invisible Power* by Genevieve Behrend (1881–1960) reenergized my search.

This short, powerful book, first published in 1921, also led me to attempt a new exercise, which I want to share with you as something to personally try. I take individual experimentation very seriously. That's why I call myself a "believing historian." As Behrend writes: "One who essays the role of a messenger of psychological truths can only be convincing as he or she has tested them in the laboratory of personal mental experience."

Before I get to my suggested exercise, however, let me call attention to an important idea found in Behrend's opening chapter. The author and metaphysical seeker—a close student of New Thought pioneer Thomas Troward (1847–1916)—provides a clarifying portrait of her mind-power principles early in this volume:

> We now fly through the air, not because anyone has been able to change the laws of Nature, but because the inventor of the flying machine learned how to apply Nature's laws and, by making orderly use of them, produced the desired result. So far as the natural forces are concerned, nothing has changed since the beginning. There were no airplanes in "the Year One," because those of that generation could not conceive the idea as a practical, working possibility. "It has not yet been done," was the argument, "and it cannot be done." Yet the laws and materials for practical flying machines existed then as now.
>
> Troward tells us that the great lesson he learned from the airplane and wireless telegraphy is the triumph of principle over precedent, the working out of an idea to its logical conclusion in spite of accumulated contrary testimony of all past experience.

This practical guidebook does not endorse the idea that your visualizing powers will "manifest" properties from the ether. (I prefer the term "select," a choice I expand on in *The Miracle Club*.) Rather, the powers of causative thought can bring about the extraordinary by working through *established channels* of creation. We do not bend natural laws, Behrend writes—we discover the multitudinous possibilities within them.

As Behrend puts it, with her emphasis in the original: "*In visualizing, or making a mental picture, you are not endeavoring to change the laws of Nature. You are fulfilling them.*"

In essence, Behrend's system is modern Hermeticism: "As above, so below." She writes that while the individual must function within the physical sphere in which he finds himself—obeying its limits and natural laws—he is also an extension of Infinite Mind, or what the Ancient Greeks called *Nous*, and functions as a channel of creative ability whose method is thought.

"Your conscious Oneness with the great Whole is the secret of success," Behrend writes.

Whether this is your first book of New Thought philosophy or whether you are a veteran reader who, like me, needs a refresher let me propose an exercise: Read this book in full at your own pace. When you are finished, select and dedicate one hour—just one hour—during which you will assume that its *every premise about thought and creation is correct*. Act as though you possess ultimate creative responsibility for your life. Entertain no doubts. This is your private experiment. Tell no one what you are doing. Behrend provides wise counsel on how speech dissipates the impact of thought: "One tells one's troubles to weaken them, to get them off one's mind, and when a thought is given out, its power is dissipated."

If your *one hour* leaves you satisfied, select another period in which to expand your experiment to two hours. Then expand two to four, four to eight, and, finally, eight to sixteen, which is, roughly, the length of a waking day. Once you reach the waking-day stage of your experiment, go to sleep visualizing a desired outcome. That final step amounts to a twenty-four-hour commitment. See what occurs. Will you try? It requires only an hour to start.

If you experience doubts or setbacks, do not worry. There is no need to start over. Life is filled with switchbacks. It is unrealistic and unnecessary to attempt to avoid them. You are not seeking an impossibly high standard of inner performance. You are simply exploring your dimensions as an ethical and creative being—and probing "your invisible power" as a self-devised being.

Since this exercise begins with a single hour, I will follow the theme of my recent work and call it . . . *The Miracle Hour*. It belongs to you. The point of New Thought is to prove its premises to oneself. Let's see what occurs together.

One final note: I ask that you read Behrend's tenth chapter with special care. In it she describes how she became a personal student of Thomas Troward, after the retired judge and metaphysical writer had first ignored and then refused her entreaties.

To attain her goal, Behrend didn't just think— she acted: with persistence, some degree of audacity, and aplomb. Her attitude and actions are a lesson in themselves. She impressed her hoped-for teacher by *her rigor of preparation*. Never neglect that. "A great idea is valueless," Behrend writes, "unless accompanied by physical action."

Allow this book to summon you to ideas—and action.

Mitch Horowitz is a PEN Award-winning historian and the author of books including *Occult America* and *The Miracle Club*. His recent G&D Media titles include *The Miracle Month* and *The Miracle Habits*. Twitter: @MitchHorowitz | Instagram: @Mitch-Horowitz23

INTRODUCTION

Genevieve Behrend was the only personal pupil that the great Thomas Troward ever had. She studied with him privately, at his home at Ruan Manor, Cornwall, England, for two years, 1912 to 1914, inclusive. She founded The School of the Builders in New York City and was the head of it until 1925. For five years thereafter she conducted the same school in Los Angeles and then toured the entire United States and Canada, presenting the Troward philosophy at its best, as only she was fully qualified to do, in almost every city of appreciable size.

She spent thirty-five years as one of America's greatest and best-known lecturers, teachers and practitioners. Millions heard and enjoyed her, not only on the public platform but over radio. Her students numbered tens of thousands all over the English-speaking world. Paris, France was her native city but she was half Scotch. This little book, *Your Invisible Power*, was her first. However it remains the most popular of all her books and has been, since its first edition, one of the world's best sellers on Mental Science. It has exhausted scores of editions.

Herein, Genevieve Behrend presents the Troward philosophy at its best, in her incomparable simple, direct and dynamic manner so well known to so many. Although she has written several other books this one remains her masterpiece.

—WORTH SMITH

Publisher's Note: Worth Smith, prominent author and authority on the Great Pyramid, has been the husband and closest collaborator of Genevieve Behrend for twenty-two years.

FOREWORD

These pages have been written for the purpose of furnishing you a key to the attainment of your desires, and to explain that Fear should be entirely banished from your consciousness in order for you to obtain possession of the things you want.

This pre-supposes, of course, that your desire for possession is based upon your aspiration for greater happiness. For example, you feel that the possession of more money, lands, or friends will make you happier, and your desire for possession of these things arises from a conviction that their possession will bring you freedom and contentment. In your effort to possess, you will discover that the thing you most need is to consistently "Be" your best self.

One morning after class a man came to me and asked if I would speak the word of supply for him, as he was sadly in the need of money. He offered me a $5 bill with the remark: "Dear Madam, that is half of every dollar I have in the world. I am in debt; my wife and child have not the proper clothing; in fact, I must have money." I explained to him that money was the symbol of differentiated substance, that this substance filled all space, that it was present for him at that very moment, and would manifest to him as the money he required. "But," he questioned, "it may come too late." I told him it could not come too late, as it was eternally present. He understood and got the uplift of my spoken word.

I did not see the man again, but six months later I had a letter from him stating he was in New Orleans. He said, "I am well established here in my regular profession of photography; I own my own home, have an automobile of my own, and am generally prospering. And dear Mrs. Behrend, I want to thank you for lifting me out of the depths that day in New York.

"Three days after I talked to you, a man whom I have not seen for years met me on the street. When

I explained my situation to him, he loaned me the money to pay my bills and come down here. The enclosed check is to help you continue your wonderful work of teaching people how to mentally reach out and receive their never-failing supply. I would not take anything for my understanding as you have given it to me. God bless you."

A feeling that greater possessions, no matter of what kind they may be, will of *themselves* bring contentment or happiness, is a misunderstanding. No person, place, or thing can give you happiness. They may give you cause for happiness and a feeling of contentment, but the Joy of Living comes from within.

Therefore, it is here recommended that you should make the effort to obtain the things which you feel will bring you joy, provided that your desires are in accord with the Joy of Living.

It is also desired, in this volume, to suggest the possibilities in store for all who make persistent effort to understand the Law of Visualization, and who make practical application of this knowledge on whatever plane they may be. The word "effort," as here employed, is not intended to convey the idea of strain. All study and meditation should be without strain or tension.

It has been my endeavor to show that by starting at the beginning of the creative action, or mental picture, certain corresponding results are sure to follow. "While the laws of the Universe cannot be altered, they can be made to work under specific conditions, thereby producing results for individual advancement which cannot be obtained under the spontaneous workings of the law provided by Nature."

However far these suggestions I have given—of the possibilities in store for you, through visualizing, may carry you beyond your past experience, they nowhere break the continuity of the law of cause and effect.

If through the suggestions here given, any one is brought to realize that his mind is a center through and in which "all power there is" is in operation, simply waiting to be given direction in the one and only way through which it can take specific action—and this means reaction in concrete or physical form—then the mission to which this book is dedicated has been fulfilled.

Try to remember that the picture you think, feel, and see is reflected into the Universal Mind, and by the natural law of reciprocal action must return to you in either spiritual or physical form. Knowledge of this law of reciprocal action between the individual and the Universal Mind opens to you free access to all you may wish to *possess* or to *be*.

It must be steadfastly borne in mind that all this can be true only for the individual who recognizes that he derives his power to make an abiding mental picture from the All-Originating Universal Spirit of Life, and can be used constructively only so long as it is employed and retained in harmony with the nature of the Spirit which originated it. To insure this there must be no inversion of the thought of the individual regarding his relationship to this Universal Originating Spirit, which is that of a son, through which the parent mind acts and reacts.

Thus conditioned, whatever you think and feel yourself to be, the Creative Spirit of Life is bound to faithfully reproduce in a corresponding reaction. This is the great reason for picturing yourself and your affairs the way you wish them to be as existing facts—though invisible to the physical eye—and living in your picture. An honest endeavor to do this, always recognizing that your own mind is a projection of the Originating Spirit, will prove to you that the best there is, is yours in all your ways.

—G.B.

Los Angeles, California;
May, 1929.

CHAPTER ONE

Order of Visualization

The exercise of the visualizing faculty keeps your mind in order, and attracts to you the things you need to make life more enjoyable in an orderly way.

If you train yourself in the practice of deliberately picturing your desire and carefully examining your picture, you will soon find that your thoughts and desires proceed in a more orderly procession than ever before.

Having reached a state of ordered mentality, you are no longer in a constant state of mental hurry. Hurry is Fear, and consequently destructive.

In other words, when your understanding grasps the power to visualize your heart's desire and hold it with your will, it attracts to you all things requisite to the fulfillment of that picture by the harmonious vibrations of the law of attraction.

You realize that since Order is Heaven's first law, and visualization places things in their natural order, then it must be a heavenly thing to visualize.

Everyone visualizes, whether he knows it or not. Visualizing is the great secret of success.

The conscious use of this great power attracts to you multiplied resources, intensifies your wisdom, and enables you to make use of advantages which you formerly failed to recognize.

A lady once came to me for help in selling a piece of property. After I explained to her just how to make a mental picture of the sale, going through the details mentally, exactly as she would do if the property were sold, she came a week later and told me how one day she was walking along the street, when the thought suddenly occurred to her to go and see a certain real estate dealer, to whom she had not yet been.

She hesitated for a moment when she first got the idea, as it seemed to her that that man could not sell her property. However, upon the strength of what I had told her, she followed the lead and went to the real estate man, who sold the property for her in just three days after she had first approached him. This was simply following along with the natural law of demand and supply.

We now fly through the air, not because anyone has been able to change the laws of Nature, but because the inventor of the flying machine learned how to apply Nature's laws and, by making orderly use of them, produced the desired result. So far as the natural forces are concerned, nothing has changed since the beginning. There were no airplanes in "the Year One," because those of that generation could not conceive the idea as a practical, working possibility. "It has not yet been done," was the argument, "and it cannot be done." Yet the laws and materials for practical flying machines existed then as now.

Troward tells us that the great lesson he learned from the airplane and wireless telegraphy is the triumph of principle over precedent, the working out of an idea to its logical conclusion in spite of accumulated contrary testimony of all past experience.

With such an example before you, you must realize that there are still greater secrets to be disclosed. Also, "That you hold the key within yourself, with which to unlock the secret chamber that contains your heart's desire.

"All that is necessary in order that you may use this key and make your life exactly what you wish it to be, is a careful inquiry into the unseen causes which stand back of every external and visible condition. Then bring these unseen causes into harmony with your conception, and you will find that you can make practical working realities of possibilities which at present seem but fantastic dreams."

A woman came to me in New York City, asking for help, as she was out of work. I spoke the word of ever-present supply for her and intensified it by mentally seeing the woman in the position she dreamed of, but which she had been unable to make a practical reality.

That same afternoon she telephoned and said she could hardly believe her senses, as she had just taken exactly the kind of a position she wanted. The employer told her she had been wanting a woman like her for months.

We all knew that the balloon was the forefather of the airplane. In 1766 Henry Cavendish, an English nobleman, proved that hydrogen gas was seven times lighter than air. From that discovery the balloon came into existence, and from the ordinary balloon the dirigible, a cigar-shaped airship, was evolved.

Study of aeronautics and laws of the aerial locomotion of birds and projectiles led to the belief that mechanism could be evolved by which heavier-than-air machines could be made to travel from place to place and remain in the air by the maintenance of great speed, which would overcome by propulsive force the ordinary law of gravitation. Professor Langley of Washington, who developed much of the theory which others afterward improved upon, was subjected to much derision when he sent a model airplane up, only to have it bury its nose in the muddy waters of the Potomac. But the Wright Brothers, who experimented later, realized the possibility of traveling through the air in a machine that had no gas bag. They *saw* themselves enjoying this mode of transportation with great facility. It is said that one of the brothers would tell the other, when their varied experiences did not turn out as they expected: "It's all right, Brother, I can *see* myself riding in that machine, and it travels easily and steadily."

Those Wright Brothers knew what they wanted and kept their pictures constantly before them. Now transportation through the air is developing rapidly and we all feel sure it will in the near future become as ordinary a method of travel as the automobile.

In visualizing, or making a mental picture, you are not endeavoring to change the laws of Nature. You are fulfilling them.

Your object in visualizing is to bring things into regular order, both mentally and physically. When you realize that this method of employing the Creative Power brings your desires, one after another, into practical, material accomplishment, your confidence in the mysterious but unfailing law of attraction, which has its central power station in the very heart of your word-picture, becomes supreme. Nothing can shake it. You never feel that it is necessary to take anything from anybody else. You have learned that asking and seeking have, as their correlatives, receiving and finding. You know that all you have to do is to start the plastic substance of the Universe flowing into the thought-moulds your picture-desire provides.

CHAPTER
TWO

How to Attract to Yourself the Things You Desire

The power within you which enables you to form a thought-picture is the starting point of all there is. In its original state it is the undifferentiated formless substance of life. Your thought-picture makes the model, so to say, into which this form-less substance takes shape.

Visualizing, or mentally seeing things and conditions as you wish them to be, is the condensing, the specializing power in you which might be illustrated by comparison with the lens of a magic lantern, which is one of the best symbols of the imaging faculty.

It illustrates the idea of the working of the Creative Spirit on the plane of initiative and selection—or in its concentrated, specializing form—in a remarkably clear manner.

The picture slide illustrates your own mental picture—invisible in the lantern of your mind until you turn on the light of your will.

That is to say, you light up your desire with absolute faith that the Creative Spirit of Life, in you, is doing the work. By the steady flow of the light of the Will on the Spirit, your desired picture is projected upon the screen of the physical world—an exact reproduction of the pictured slide in your mind.

A woman came to me for help to cause her husband to return to her. She said she was very unhappy and lonely without him and longed to be reunited. I told her she could not lose love and protection, because both belonged to her. She asked what she should do to get her husband back again. I told her to follow the great power of intuition and think of her husband as perfectly free, and the embodiment of all that a husband should be.

She went away quite happy, but returned in a few days to tell me that her husband desired a divorce in order to marry again. She was quite agitated and had evidently relaxed her will in following the instructions given at the former interview. Again I told her to hold constantly in her mind that the loving protection of the Spirit of Life would guide her in perfect happiness.

A month later she came again and said that her husband had married the other woman. This time she had completely lost her mental grip. I repeated the words for her as before, and she regained her poise. Two months later she came back to me, full of joy. Her husband had come to her, begging her forgiveness, and telling her what a terrible mistake he had made, as he could not be happy without her. They are now living happily together, and she, at least, learned the necessity of holding her pictured desire steadily in place by the use of her will.

Visualizing without a will sufficiently steady to inhibit every thought and feeling contrary to your pictured thought would be as useless as a magic lantern without the light.

On the other hand, if your will is sufficiently developed to hold your picture in thought and feeling, without any "ifs"; simply realizing that your thought is the great attracting power, then your mental picture is as certain to be projected upon your physical world as a picture slide put into a magic lantern shows on the screen.

Try projecting the picture in a magic lantern with a light that is constantly shifting from one side to the other, and you will produce the effect of an uncertain will. It is as necessary that you should always have back of your picture a strong, steady will, as it is to have a strong steady light back of a picture slide.

The joyous assurance with which you make your picture is the very powerful magnet of Faith, and nothing can obliterate it. You are happier than you ever were, because you have learned to know where your source of supply is, and you rely upon its never-failing response to the direction you give it.

All said and done, happiness is the one thing which every human being wants, and the study of visualization enables you to get more out of life than you ever enjoyed before. Increasing possibilities keep opening out, more and more, before you.

A businessman once told me that since practicing visualization, and forming the habit of devoting a few minutes each day to thinking about his work as he desired it to be, in a large, broad way, his orders had more than doubled in six months.

His method was to go into a room every morning before breakfast and take a mental inventory of his business as he had left it the evening before, and then enlarge upon it. He said he expanded and expanded in this way, until his affairs were in a remarkably successful condition. He would see himself in his office doing everything he wanted done. His occupation required him to meet many strangers every day.

In his mental picture he saw himself meeting these people, understanding their needs, and supplying them in just the way they wished. This habit, he said, had strengthened and steadied his will in an almost inconceivable manner.

Furthermore, by thus mentally seeing things as he wished them to be, he had acquired the confident feeling that a certain Creative Power was exercising itself, for him and through him, for the purpose of improving his little world.

When you first begin to visualize seriously, you may feel, as many others do, that someone else may be forming the same picture you are, and that, naturally, would not suit your purpose. Do not give yourself any concern about this.

Simply try to realize that your picture is an orderly exercise of the Universal Creative Power specifically applied. Then you may be sure that no one can work in opposition to you. The universal law of harmony prevents that.

Endeavor to bear in mind that your mental picture is Universal Mind specifically exercising its inherent powers of initiative and selection.

God, or Universal Mind, made man for the special purpose of differentiating Himself through him. Everything there is, came into existence in this same way, by this self-same law of self-differentiation, and for the same purpose. First came the idea, the mental picture, or the prototype of the thing, which is the thing itself in its incipiency.

The Great Architect of the Universe contemplated Himself as manifesting through his polar opposite—matter—and the idea expanded and projected itself until we have not only a world, but many worlds.

Many people ask, "But why should we have a physical world at all?" The answer is: "Because it is the nature of Originating Substance to solidify, under directivity rather than activity, just as it is the nature of wax to harden when it becomes cold, or plaster of Paris to become firm and solid when exposed to the air."

Your picture is this same Divine Substance in its original state, taking form through the individualized center of Divine operation, in your mind; and there is no power to prevent this combination of Spiritual Substance from becoming physical form. It is the nature of Spirit to complete its work, and an idea is not complete until it has made for itself a vehicle.

Nothing can prevent your picture from coming into concrete form except the same power which gave it birth—yourself.

Suppose you wish to have a more orderly room. You look about your room, and the idea of order suggests boxes, closets, shelves, hooks, and so forth. The box, the closet and the hooks, are all concrete ideas of order, because they are the vehicles through which order and harmony suggest themselves.

CHAPTER
THREE

Relation Between Mental and Physical Form

Some persons feel that it is not quite proper to visualize for *things*. "It's too material," they say. Why, material form is necessary for the self-recognition of Spirit from the individual standpoint, and this is the means through which the Creative Process is carried forward.

Therefore, far from matter being an illusion and something which ought not to be, matter is the necessary channel for the self-differentiation of Spirit.

However, it is not my desire to lead you into lengthy and tiresome scientific reasoning, in order to remove the mystery from visualization and to put it upon a logical foundation.

Naturally, each individual will do this in his own way. My only wish is to point out to you the easiest way I know, which is the road on which Troward guides me. I feel sure you will conclude, as I have, that the only mystery in connection with visualizing is the mystery of life taking form, governed by unchangeable and easily understood laws.

We all possess more power and greater possibilities than we realize, and visualizing is one of the greatest of these powers, it brings other Possibilities to our observation. When we pause to think for a moment, we realize that for a cosmos to exist at all, it must be the outcome of a Cosmic Mind, which binds "all individual minds to a certain generic unity of action, thereby producing all things as realities and nothing as illusions." If you will take this thought of Troward's and meditate upon it without prejudice, you will surely realize that concrete material form is an absolute necessity of the Creative Process; also "that matter is not an illusion but a necessary channel thru which life differentiates itself." If you consider matter in its right order, as the polar opposite to Spirit, you will not find any antagonism between them. On the contrary, together they constitute one harmonious whole. And when you realize this, you feel, in your practice of visualizing, that you are working from cause to effect, from beginning to end. In reality your mental picture is the specialized outworking of the Originating Spirit. One could talk for hours on purely scientific lines, showing, as Troward says, "that raw material for the formation of the solar systems is universally distributed throughout all space. Yet investigation shows that while the Heavens are studded with millions of suns, there are spaces which show no signs of cosmic activity. This being true, There must be something which started cosmic activity in certain places, while passing over others in which the raw material was equally available. At first thought, one might attribute development of cosmic energy to the etheric particles themselves. Upon investigation however, we find that this is mathematically impossible in a medium which is equally distributed throughout space, for all its particles are in equilibrium; therefore, no one particle possesses in itself a greater power of originating motion than the other. Thus we find that the initial movement, though working in and through the particles of primary substance, is not the particles themselves. It is this something we mean when we speak of Spirit."

This same power that brought universal substance into existence will bring your individual thought or mental picture into physical form. There is no difference in the power. The only difference is a difference of degree. The power and the substance themselves are the same. Only in working out your mental picture, it has transferred its creative energy from the Universal to the particular, and is working in the same unfailing manner from its specific center, your mind.

CHAPTER FOUR

Operation of Your Mental Picture

The operation of a large telephone system may be used as a simile. The main, or head central subdivides itself into many branch centrals, every branch being in direct connection with the main central, and each individual branch recognizing the source of its existence, reports all things to its central head. Therefore, when assistance of any nature is required: new supplies, difficult repairs to be done, or what not, the branch in need goes at once to its central head. It would not think of referring its difficulties (or its successes) to the main central of a telegraph system, though they might belong to the same organization. These different branch centrals know that the only remedy for any difficulty must come from the central out of which they were projected and to which they are always attached.

If we, as individual branches of the Universal Mind, would refer our difficulties in the same confident manner to the source from which we were projected, and use the remedies which it has provided, we would realize what Jesus meant when he said, "Ask and ye shall receive." Our every requirement would be met. Surely the Father must supply the child. The trunk of the tree cannot fail to provide for its branches.

A man came to me in great distress, saying he was about to lose his home in the South. In his own words, it was mortgaged to the hilt, and his creditors were going to foreclose. It was the house in which he had been born and had grown to young manhood, and the thought of losing it filled his heart and mind with sorrow, not only from a money standpoint, but from the standpoint of sentimental association. I explained to him that the Power that brought him into existence did so for the purpose of expressing its limitless supply through him; that there was no power on earth which could cut him off from his source except his own consciousness, and that in reality he would not be cut off then. I explained to him that he had it, but was unable to recognize that it was there, and said to him, "Infinite substance is manifesting in you right now." The next week, on Sunday, just before leaving my dressing room in the Selwyn Theatre to give my afternoon message, I received the following note: "Dear Mrs. Behrend: I want you to know that I am the happiest man in the whole city of New York. My home in the South is saved. The money came in the most miraculous way, and I have telegraphed enough to pay off the mortgage. Please tell the people this afternoon about this wonderful Power."

You may be sure I did, explaining to them that everything animate or inanimate is called into existence or outstandingness by a Power which itself does not stand out. The Power which creates the mental picture—the Originating Spirit Substance of your pictured desire—does not stand out. It projects the substance of itself, which is a solidified counterpart of itself, while it—the Power—remains invisible to the physical eye. Those will appreciate the value of visualizing who are able to realize Paul's meaning when he said, "The worlds were formed by the word of God. Things which are seen are not made of things which do appear."

There is nothing unusual or mysterious in the idea of your pictured desire coming into material evidence. It is the working of a universal, natural Law. The world was projected by the self-contemplation of the Universal Mind, and this same action is taking place in its individualized branch which is the Mind of Man. Everything in the whole world, from the hat on your head to the boots on your feet, has its beginning in mind and comes into existence in exactly the same manner. All are projected thoughts, solidified. Your personal advance in evolution depends on your right use of the power of visualizing, and your use of it depends on whether you recognize that you, yourself, are a particular center through and in which the Originating Spirit is finding ever new expression for potentialities already existing within Itself. This is evolution.

Your mental picture is the force of attraction which evolves and combines the Originating Substance into specific shape. Your picture is the combining and evolving power house, in a generative sense, so to say, through which the Originating Creative Spirit expresses itself. Its creative action is limitless, without beginning and without end, and always progressive and orderly. "It proceeds stage by stage, each stage being a necessary preparation for the one to follow." Now let us see if we can get an idea of the different stages by which the things in the world have come to be. Troward says, "If we can get at the working principle which is producing these results, we can very quickly and easily give it personal application. First, we find that the thought of Originating Life, or Spirit, concerning Itself is its simple awareness of its own being, and this, demanding a relationship to something else, produces a primary ether, a universal substance out of which everything in the world must grow."

Troward also tells us that "though this awareness of being is a necessary foundation for any further possibilities, it is not much to talk about." It is the same with individualized Spirit, which is yourself. Before you can entertain the idea of making a mental picture of your desire as being at all practical, you must have some idea of your being; of your "I am"; and just as soon as you are conscious of your "I-amness," you begin to wish to enjoy the freedom which this consciousness suggests. You want to do more and be more, and as you fulfill this desire within yourself, localized spirit begins conscious activities in you. The thing you are more concerned with is the specific action of the Creative Spirit of Life, Universal Mind specialized. The localized God-germ in you is your personality, your individuality and since the joy of absolute freedom is the inherent nature of this God-germ, it is natural that it should endeavor to enjoy itself through its specific center. And as you grow in the comprehension that your being, your individuality, is God particularizing Himself, you naturally develop Divine tendencies. You want to enjoy life and liberty. You want freedom in your affairs as well as in your consciousness, and it is natural that you should. With this progressive wish there is always a faint thought-picture. As your wish and your recognition grow into an intense desire, this desire becomes a clear mental picture. For example, a young lady studying music wishes she had a piano in order to practice at home. She wants the piano so much that she can mentally see it in one of the rooms. She holds the picture of the piano and indulges in the mental reflection of the pleasure and advantage it will be to have the piano in the corner of the living room. One day she finds it there, just as she had pictured it.

As you grow in understanding as to who you are, where you came from, what the purpose of your being is, and how you are to fulfill the purpose for which you are intended, you will become a more and more perfect center through which the Creative Spirit of Life can enjoy itself. And you will realize that there can be but one creative process filling all space, which is the same in its potentiality whether universal or individual. Furthermore, all there is, whether on the plane of the visible or invisible, had its origin in the localized action of thought, or a mental picture, and this includes yourself, because you are Universal Spirit localized, and the same creative action is taking place through you.

Now you are no doubt asking yourself why there is so much sickness and misery in the world. If the same power and intelligence which brought the world into existence is in operation in the mind of man, why does it not manifest itself as strength joy, health and plenty? If one can have one's desires fulfilled by simply making a mental picture of that desire, holding on to it with the will, and without anxiety, doing on the outward plane whatever seems necessary to bring the desire into fulfillment, then there seems no reason for the existence of sickness and poverty. Surely no one desires either. The first reason is that few persons will take the trouble to inquire into the working principle of the Laws of Life. If they did, they would soon convince themselves that there is no necessity for the sickness and poverty which we see about us. They would realize that visualizing is a principle and not a fallacy. There are a few who have found it worth while to study this simple, though absolutely unfailing law, which will deliver them from bondage. However, the race as a whole is not willing to give the time required for the study. It is either too simple, or too difficult. They may make a picture of their desire with some little understanding of visualizing for a day or two, but more frequently it is for an hour or so.

If you will insist upon mentally seeing yourself surrounded by things and conditions as you wish them to be you will understand that the Creative Energy sends its substance in the direction indicated by the tendency of your thoughts. Herein lies the advantage of holding your thought in the form of a mental picture.

A man in the hardware business in New Jersey came to me in great distress. He would have to go into bankruptcy unless something happened in a fortnight. He said he had never heard of visualizing. I explained to him how to make a mental picture of his business increasing, instead of a picture of losing it. In about a month's time he returned very happy and told me how he had succeeded. He said, "I have my debts all paid, and my shop is full of new supplies." His business was then on a solid basis. It was beautiful to see his Faith.

The more enthusiasm and faith you are able to put into your picture, the more quickly it will come into visible form, and your enthusiasm is increased by keeping your desire secret. The moment you speak it to any living soul, that moment your power is weakened. Your power, your magnet of attraction is not that strong, and consequently cannot reach so far. The more perfectly a secret between your mind and your outer self is guarded, the more vitality you give your power of attraction. One tells one's troubles to weaken them, to get them off one's mind, and when a thought is given out, its power is dissipated. Talk it over with yourself, and even write it down, then destroy the paper.

However, this does not mean that you should strenuously endeavor to compel the Power to work out your picture on the special lines that you think it should. That method would soon exhaust you and hinder the fulfillment of your purpose. A wealthy relative need not necessarily die, or someone lose a fortune on the street, to materialize the $10,000 which you are mentally picturing. One of the doormen in the building in which I lived heard much of the mental picturing of desires from visitors passing out of my rooms. The average desire was for $500. He considered that five dollars was more in his line and began to visualize it, without the slightest idea of where or how he was to get it. My parrot flew out of the window, and I telephoned to the men in the courtyard to get it for me. One caught it, and it bit him on the finger. The doorman, who had gloves on, and did not fear a similar hurt, took hold of it and brought it up to me. I gave him five one dollar bills for his service. This sudden reward surprised him. He enthusiastically told me that he had been visualizing for just $5, merely from hearing that others visualized. He was delighted at the unexpected realization of his mental picture.

All you have to do is to make such a mental picture of your heart's desire, and hold it cheerfully in place with your will, always conscious that the same Infinite Power which brought the universe into existence, brought you into form for the purpose of enjoying Itself in and through you. And since it is all Life, Love, Light, Power, Peace, Beauty, and Joy, and is the only Creative Power there is, the form it takes in and through you depends upon the direction given it by your thought. In you it is undifferentiated, waiting to take any direction given it as it passes through the instrument which it has made for the purpose of self-distribution—you.

It is this Power which enables you to transfer your thoughts from one form to another. The power to change your mind is the individualized Universal Power taking the initiative, giving direction to the unformed substance contained in every thought.

It is the simplest thing in the world to give this highly sensitive Substance any form you will, through visualizing. Anyone can do it with a small expenditure of effort. Once you really believe that your mind is a center through which the unformed substance of all there is in your world, takes involuntary form, the only reason your picture does not always materialize is because you have introduced something antagonistic to the fundamental principle. Very often this destructive element is caused by the frequency with which you change your pictures. After many such changes, you decide that your original desire is what you want after all. Upon this conclusion, you begin to wonder why it (being your first picture) has not materialized. The Substance with which you are mentally dealing is more sensitive than the most sensitive photographer's film. If, while taking a picture, you suddenly remembered you had already taken a picture on that same plate, you would not expect a perfect result of either picture. On the other hand, you may have taken two pictures on the same plate unconsciously. When the plate has been developed, and the picture comes into physical view, you do not condemn the principle of photography, nor are you puzzled to understand why your picture has turned out so unsatisfactorily. You do not feel that it is impossible for you to obtain a good, clear picture of the subject in question. You know that you can do so, by simply starting at the beginning, putting in a new plate, and determining to be more careful while taking your picture next time. If these lines are followed out, you are sure of a satisfactory result. If you will proceed in the same manner with your mental picture, doing your part in a correspondingly confident frame of mind, the result will be just as perfect. The laws of visualizing are as infallible as the laws governing photography. In fact, photography is the outcome of visualizing.

Again, your results in visualizing the fulfillment of your desires may be imperfect, and your desires delayed, through the misuse of this power, owing to the thought that the fulfillment of your desire is contingent upon certain persons or conditions. The Originating Principle is not in any way dependent upon any person, place, or thing. It has no past and knows no future. The law is that the Originating Creative Principle of Life is "the universal here and everlasting now." It creates its own vehicles through which to operate. Therefore, past experience has no bearing upon your present picture. So do not try to obtain your desire through a channel which may not be natural for it, even though it may seem reasonable to you. Your feeling should be that the thing, or the consciousness, which you so much desire, is normal and natural, a part of yourself, a form of your evolution. If you can do this, there is no power to prevent your enjoying the fulfillment of the picture you have in mind, or any other you may create.

CHAPTER FIVE

Expressions from Beginners

Hundreds of persons have realized that "visualizing is an Aladdin's lamp to him with a mighty will." General Foch says that his feelings were so outraged during the Franco-Prussian war in 1870 that he visualized himself leading a French army against the Germans to victory. He said he made his picture, smoked his pipe, and waited. This is one result of visualizing with which we are all familiar.

A famous actress wrote a long article in one of the leading Sunday papers last winter, describing how she rid herself of excessive avoirdupois by seeing her figure constantly as she wished to be.

A very interesting letter came to me from a doctor's wife, while I was lecturing in New York. She began with the hope that I would never discontinue my lectures on visualization, which were helping humanity to realize the wonderful fact that they possessed the means of liberation within themselves. Relating her own experience, she said that she was born on the East Side of New York in the poorest quarter. From earliest girlhood she had cherished a dream of marrying a physician some day. This dream gradually formed a stationary mental picture. The first position she obtained was in the capacity of a maid in a physician's family. Leaving this place, she entered the family of another doctor. The wife of her employer died, and in the doctor married her—the result of long-pictured yearning. After that, both and her husband conceived the idea of owning a fruit farm in the South. They formed a mental picture of the idea and put their faith in its eventual fulfillment. The letter she sent me came from her fruit farm in the South. Her second mental picture had seen the light of materialization.

Many letters of a similar nature come to me every day. The following is a case that was printed in the New York Herald last May:

"Atlantic City, May 5—She was an old woman, and when she was arraigned before Judge Clarence

Goldenberg in the police court today she was so weak and tired she could hardly stand. The Judge asked the court attendant what she was charged with. 'Stealing a bottle of milk, Your Honor,' repeated the officer. 'She took it from the door-step of a downtown cottage before daybreak this morning.' 'Why did you do that?' Judge Goldenberg asked her. 'I was hungry,' the old woman said. 'I didn't have a cent in the world and no way to get anything to eat except to steal it. I didn't think anybody would mind if I took a bottle of milk.' 'What's your name?' asked the judge. 'Weinberg,' said the old woman, 'Elizabeth Weinberg.' Judge Goldenberg asked her a few questions about herself. Then he said: 'Well, you're not very wealthy now, but you're no longer poor. I've been searching for you for months. I've got $500 belonging to you from the estate of a relative. I am the executor of the estate.'

"Judge Goldenberg paid the woman's fine out of his own pocket, and then escorted her into his office, where he turned her legacy over to her and sent a policeman out to find her a lodging place."

I learned later that this little woman bad been desiring and mentally picturing $500, while all the time ignorant of how it could possibly come to her. But she kept her vision and strengthened it with her faith.

In an issue of Good Housekeeping there was an article by Addington Bruce entitled "Stiffening Your Mental Backbone." It is very instructive, and would benefit anyone to read it. He says, in part: "Form the habit of devoting a few moments every day to thinking about your work in a large, broad, imaginative way, as a vital necessity to yourself and a useful service to society."

James J. Hill, the great railway magnate, before he started building his road from coast to coast, said that he took hundreds of trips all along the line before there was a rail laid. It is said that he would sit for hours with a map of the United States before him and mentally travel from coast to coast, just as we do now over his fulfilled mental picture. It would be possible to call your attention to hundreds of similar cases.

The method of picturing to yourself what you desire is both simple and enjoyable, if you once understand the principle back of it well enough to believe it. Over and above everything else, be sure of what it is you really want. Then specialize your desire along the lines given in the following chapter.

CHAPTER
SIX

Suggestions for Making Your Mental Picture

Perhaps you want to feel that you've lived to some purpose. You want to be contented and happy; you feel that good health and a successful business would give you contentment. After you have decided once and for all that this is what you want, you proceed to picture yourself healthy, and your business just as great a success as you can naturally conceive it growing into. The best times for making your definite picture are just before breakfast, and again, before retiring at night. As it is necessary to give yourself plenty of time,it may be necessary to rise earlier than you usually do. Go into a room where you will not be disturbed, meditate for a few moments upon the practical working of the law of visualizing, and ask yourself, "How did the things about me first come into existence? How can I get more quickly in touch with my invisible supply?"

Someone felt that comfort would be better expressed and experienced by sitting on a chair than on the floor. So the very beginning of a chair was the desire to be at ease. With this came the picture of some sort of a chair, The same principle applies to the hat and the clothes you wear. Go carefully into the thought of the principle back of the thing. Establish it as a personal experience; make it a fact to your consciousness. Then open a window, take about ten deep breaths, and during the time draw a large imaginary circle of light pound you. As you inhale—keeping yourself in the center of this circle of light—see great rays of light coming from the circle and entering your body at all points, centralizing itself at your solar plexus. Hold the breath a few moments at this central point of your body—the solar plexus—then slowly exhale. As you do this, mentally see imaginary rays, or sprays, of light going up through the body, and down and out through feet. Mentally spray your entire body with this imaginary light. When you have finished the breathing exercise, sit in a comfortable upright chair and mentally know there is but one Life, one Substance, and this Life Substance of the Universe is finding pleasure in self-recognition in you. Repeat some affirmation of this kind, until you feel the truth and stimulating reality of the words which you are affirming. Then begin your picture. If you are thorough in this, you will find yourself in the deep consciousness beneath the surface of your own thought power.

Whether your desire is for a state of consciousness, or a possession, large or small, begin at the beginning. If you want a house, begin by seeing yourself in the kind of house you desire. Go all through it, taking careful note of the rooms, where the windows are situated, and such other details as help you to feel the reality of your picture. You might change some of the furniture about and look into some of the mirrors just to see how healthy, wealthy, and happy you look. Go over your picture again and again, until you feel the reality of it, then write it all down just as you have seen it, with the feeling that:

"The best there is, is mine. There is no limit to me, because my mind is a center of divine operation," and your picture is as certain to come true, in your physical world, as the sun is to shine.

CHAPTER SEVEN

Things to Remember in Using Your Thought Power for the Production of New Conditions

In Using Your Thought Power for the Production of New Conditions

1. Be sure to know exactly what conditions wish to produce. Then weigh carefully what further results the accomplishment of your desire will lead to.

2. By letting your thought dwell upon a mental picture, you are concentrating the Creative Action of Spirit in this center, where its forces are equally balanced.

3. Visualizing brings your objective mind into a state of equilibrium, which enables you to consciously direct the flow of Spirit to a definitely recognized purpose, and to carefully guard your thoughts from including a flow in the opposite direction.

4. You must always bear in mind that you are dealing with a wonderful potential energy, which is not yet differentiated into any particular form, and that by the action of your mind, you can differentiate it into any specific form that you will. Your picture assists you to keep your mind fixed on the fact that the inflow of this Creative Energy is taking place. Also, by your mental picture, you are determining the direction you wish the sensitive Creative Power to take, and by doing this, you make the externalization of your picture a certainty.

5. Remember when you are visualizing properly that there is no strenuous effort to hold your thought-forms in place. Strenuous effort defeats your purpose, and suggests the consciousness of

an adverse force to be fought against, and this creates conditions adverse to your picture.

6. By holding your picture in a cheerful frame of mind, you shut out all thoughts that would disperse or dissipate the spiritual nucleus of your picture. Because the law is Creative in its action, your pictured desire is certain of accomplishment.

7. The seventh and great thing to remember in visualizing is that you are making a mental picture for the purpose of determining the quality you are giving to the previously undifferentiated substance and energy, rather than to arrange the specific circumstances for its manifestation. That is the work of Creative Power itself. It will build its own forms of expression quite naturally, if you will allow it, and save you a great deal of needless anxiety. What you really want is expansion in a certain direction, whether of health, wealth, or what not, and so long as you get it—as you surely will, if you confidently hold to your picture—what does it matter whether it reaches by some channel which you thought you could count upon, or through some other of whose existence you had no idea. You are concentrating energy of a particular kind for a particular purpose. Keep this

in mind and let specific details take care of themselves, and never mention what you are doing to anyone.

Remember always, that "Nature, from her clearly visible surface to her most arcane depths, is one vast storehouse of light and good entirely devoted to your individual use." Your conscious Oneness with the great Whole is the secret of success, and when once you have fathomed this, you can enjoy your possession of the whole, or a part of it, at will, because by your recognition you have made it, and can increasingly make it, yours.

Never forget that every physical thing, whether for you or against you, was a sustained thought before it was a thing. Thought, as thought, is neither good nor bad; it is Creative Action and always takes physical form. Therefore, the thoughts you dwell upon become the things you possess or do not possess.

A man came to me telling me how be longed to marry a certain young woman, but felt he could not afford to as his salary was small, and work uncertain. I spoke the word of ever-present Certain, Unlimited Supply and explained that Love knows no failure.

"It is yours to enjoy. See yourself in the kind of a home you both want. Do your part, keep on loving the girl, and believe absolutely in that which Lives and Loves in you."

A few months later they both came to my study looking radiantly happy. I knew they were married. The wife said to me: "Dear Mrs. Behrend, we are very happy because we now know how to use our thought power and hold our consciousness as one, with all we want."

So be yourself and enjoy Life in your own Divine way. Do not fear to be your true self, for everything you want, wants you.

CHAPTER EIGHT

Why I Took Up the Study of Mental Science

I have frequently been questioned about my reasons for taking up the study of Mental Science, and as to the results of my search, not only in the knowledge of principles, but also in the application of that knowledge for the development of my own life.

Such inquiries are justifiable, because one who essays the role of a messenger of psychological truths can only be convincing as he or she has tested them in the laboratory of personal mental experience. This is particularly true in my case, as the only personal pupil of Judge Troward, the great Master in Mental Science, whose teaching is based upon the relation borne by the Individual Mind toward the Universal Creative Mind, which is the Giver of Life, and the manner in which that relation may be invoked to secure expansion and fuller expression in the individual life.

My initial impulse toward the study of Mental Science was an overwhelming sense of loneliness. In every life there must come some such experience of spiritual isolation as pervaded my life at that period. Notwithstanding the fact that each day found me in the midst of friends, surrounded by mirth and gaiety, there was a persistent feeling that I was alone in the world. I had been a widow for about three years, wandering from country to country, seeking for peace of mind.

The circumstances and surroundings of my life were such that my friends looked upon me as an unusually fortunate young woman. Although they recognized that I had sustained a great loss when my husband died, they knew that he had left me well provided for, free to go anywhere my pleasure dictated.

Yet, if my friends could have penetrated my inmost emotions, they would have found a deep sense of emptiness and isolation. This feeling inspired a spirit of unrest, which drove me on and on in fruitless search upon the outside, for that which I later learned could only be found within.

I studied Christian Science, but it gave me no solace, though fully realizing the, great work the Scientists were doing, and even having the pleasure and privilege of meeting Mrs. Eddy personally. But it was impossible for me to accept the fundamental teachings of Christian Science and make practical application of it.

When about to abandon the search for contentment and resign myself to resume a life of apparent amusement, a friend invited me to visit the great Seer and Teacher, Abdul Baha. After my interview with this most wonderful of men, my search for contentment began to take a change. He had told me that I would travel the world over seeking the truth, and when I had found it, would speak it out. The fulfillment of the statement of this Great Seer then seemed to be impossible. But it carried a measure of encouragement, and at least indicated that my former seeking had been in the wrong direction. I began in a feeble groping way to find contentment within myself, for had he not intimated that I should find the truth? That was the big thing, and about the only thing I remember of our interview.

A few days later, upon visiting the office of a New Thought practitioner, my attention was attracted to a book on his table entitled "The Edinburgh Lectures on Mental Science," by T. Troward. It interested me to see that Troward was a retired Divisional Judge from the Punjab, India. I purchased the book, thinking I would read it through that evening. Many have endeavored to do the same thing, only to find, as I did, that the book must be studied in order to be understood, and hundreds have decided, just as I did, to give it their undivided attention. After finding this treasure book, I went to the country for a few days, and while there, studied the volume as thoroughly as I could.

It seemed extremely difficult, and I decided to purchase another book of Troward's, in the hope that its study might not require so much of an effort. Upon inquiry I was told that a subsequent volume, "The Dore Lectures," was much the simpler and better of the two books. When I procured it, I found that it must also be studied. It took me weeks and months to get even a vague conception of the meaning of the first chapter of Dore, which is entitled "Entering Into the Spirit of It." I mean by this that it took me months to enter into the spirit of what I was reading.

But in the meantime a paragraph from page 26 arrested my attention, as seeming the greatest thing I had ever read. I memorized it and endeavored with all my soul to enter into the spirit of Troward's words. The paragraph reads:

"My mind is a center of Divine operation. The Divine operation is always for expansion and fuller expression, and this means the production of something beyond what has gone before, something entirely new, not included in the past experience, though proceeding out of it by an orderly sequence or growth. Therefore, since the Divine cannot change its inherent nature, it must operate in the same manner with me; consequently, in my own special world, of which I am the center, it will move forward to produce new conditions, always in advance of any that have gone before."

It took an effort on my part to memorize this paragraph, but in the endeavor toward this end, the words seemed to carry with them a certain stimulus Each repetition of the paragraph made it easier for me to enter into the spirit of it. The words expressed exactly what I had been seeking for. My one desire was for peace of mind. I found it comforting believe that the Divine operation in me could expand to fuller expression and produce more and more contentment—in fact, a peace mind and a degree of contentment greater than I had ever known. The paragraph further inspired me with deep interest to feel that the life-spark in me could bring into my life something entirely new. I did not wish to obliterate my past experience, but that was exactly what Troward said it would not do. The Divine operation would not exclude my past experience, but proceeding out of it would bring some new thing that would transcend anything that I had ever experienced before.

Meditation on these statements brought with it a certain joyous feeling. What a wonderful thing it would be if I could accept and sincerely believe, beyond all doubt, that this one statement of Troward's was true. Surely the Divine could not change its inherent nature, and since Divine life is operating in me, I must be Divinely inhabited, and the Divine in me must operate just as it operates upon the Universal plane. This meant that my whole world of circumstances, friends, and conditions would ultimately become a world of contentment and enjoyment of which "I am the center." This would all happen just as soon as I was able to control my mind and thereby provide a concrete center around which the Divine energies could play.

Surely it was worth trying for. If Troward had found this truth, why not I? The idea held me to my task. Later I determined to study with the man who bad realized and given to the world so great a statement. It had lifted me from my state of despondency. The immediate difficulty was the need for increased finances.

CHAPTER NINE

How I Attracted to Myself 20,000 Dollars

In the laboratory of experience in which my newly revealed relation to the Divine operation was to be tested, the first problem was a financial one. My income was a stipulated one quite enough for my everyday needs, but it did not seem sufficient to enable me to go comfortably to England, where Troward lived and remain for an indefinite period to study with so great a teacher as he must be. So before inquiring whether Troward took pupils, or whether I would be eligible in case he did, I began to use the paragraph I had memorized.

Daily, in fact, almost hourly, the words were in my mind: "My mind is a center of Divine operation, and Divine operation means expansion into something better than has gone before."

From the Edinburgh Lectures I had read something about the Law of Attraction, and from the Chapter on "Causes and Conditions" I had gleaned a vague idea of visualizing. So every night, before going to sleep, I made a mental picture of the desired $20,000 which seemed necessary to go and study with Troward.

Twenty imaginary $1,000 bills were counted over each night in my bedroom, and then, with the idea of more emphatically impressing my mind with the fact that this twenty thousand dollars was for the purpose of going to England and studying with Troward, I wrote out my picture, saw myself buying my steamer ticket, walking up and down the ship's deck from New York to London, and finally, saw myself accepted as Troward's pupil. This process was repeated every morning and every evening, always impressing more and more fully upon my mind Troward's memorized statement: "My mind is a center of Divine operations." I endeavored to keep this statement in the back part of my consciousness all the time, with no thought in mind of how the money might be obtained. Probably the reason why there was no thought of the avenues through which the money might reach me was because I could not possibly imagine where the $20,000 would come from. So I simply held my thought steady and let the power of attraction find its own ways and means.

One day while walking on the street, taking deep breathing exercises, the thought came:

"My mind is surely a center of Divine operation. If God fills all space, then God must be in my mind also; if I want this money to study with Troward that I may know the truth of Life, then both the money and the truth must be mine, though I am unable to feel or see the physical manifestations of either. Still," I declared, "it must be mine."

While these reflections were going on in my mind, there seemed to come up from within me the thought: "I Am all the substance there is," Then, from another channel in my brain the answer seemed to come, "Of course, that's it; everything must have its beginning in mind. The idea must contain within itself the only one and primary substance there is, and this means money as well as everything else." My mind accepted this idea, and immediately all the tension of mind and body was relaxed. There was a feeling of absolute certainty of being in touch with all the power Life has to give. All thought of money, teacher, or even my own personality, vanished in the great wave of joy which swept over my entire being. I walked on and on, with this feeling of joy steadily increasing and expanding until everything about me seemed aglow with resplendent light. Every person I passed appeared illuminated as I was. All consciousness of personality had disappeared, and in its place there came that great and almost overwhelming sense of joy and contentment.

That night when I made my picture of the twenty thousand dollars it was with an entirely changed aspect. On previous occasions, when making my mental picture, I had felt that I was waking up something within myself. This time there was no sensation of effort. I simply counted over the twenty thousand dollars. Then, in a most unexpected manner, from a source of which I had no consciousness at the time, there seemed to open a possible avenue through which the money might reach me.

At first it took great effort not to be excited. It all seemed so wonderful, so glorious, to be in touch with supply. But had not Troward cautioned his readers to keep all excitement out of their minds in the first flush of realization of union with Infinite supply, and to treat this fact as a perfectly natural result which had been reached through our demand? This was even more difficult for me than it was to hold the thought that "all the substance there is, I Am; I (idea) Am the beginning of all form, visible or invisible."

Just as soon as there appeared a circumstance which indicated the direction through which the twenty thousand dollars might come, I not only made a supreme effort to regard the indicated direction calmly as the first sprout of the seed I had sown in the absolute, but left no stone unturned to follow up that direction, thereby fulfilling my part. By so doing, one circumstance seemed naturally to lead to another, until, step by step, my desired twenty thousand dollars was secured. To keep my mind poised and free from excitement was my greatest effort.

This first concrete fruition of my study of Mental Science as expounded by Troward s book had come by a careful following of the methods he had outlined. In this connection, therefore I can offer to the reader no better gift than to quote Troward's book, "The Edinburgh Lectures," from which may be derived a complete idea of the line of action I was endeavoring to follow. In the chapter on Causes and Conditions he says:

"To get good results we must properly understand our relation to the great impersonal power we are using. It is intelligent, and we are intelligent, and the two intelligences must co-operate.) We must not fly in the face of the law expecting it to do for us what it can only do through us; and we must therefore use our intelligence with the knowledge that it is acting *as the instrument of a greater intelligence*; and because we have this knowledge we may and should cease from all anxiety as to the final result.

"In actual practice we must first form the ideal conception of our object with the definite intention of impressing it upon the Universal Mind—it is this thought that takes such thought out of the region of mere casual fancies and then affirm that our knowledge of the Law is sufficient reason for a calm expectation of a corresponding result, and that therefore all necessary conditions will come to us in due order. We can then turn to the affairs of our daily life with the calm assurance that the initial conditions are either there already or will soon come into view. If we do not at once see them, let us rest content with the knowledge that the spiritual prototype is already in existence and wait till some circumstance pointing in the desired direction begins to shop itself. It may be a very small circumstance, but it is the direction and not the magnitude which is to be taken into consideration. As soon as we see it we should regard it as the first sprouting of the seed sown in the Absolute, and do calmly, and without excitement, whatever the circumstances seem to require, and then later on we shall see that this doing will in turn lead to a further circumstance in the same direction, until we find ourselves conducted, step by step, to the accomplishment of our object. In this way the understanding of the great principle of the Law of Supply will, by repeated experiences, deliver us more and more completely out of the region of anxious thought and toilsome labor and bring us into a new world where the useful employment of all our powers, whether mental or physical, will only be an unfolding of our individuality upon the lines of its own nature, and therefore a perpetual source of health and happiness; a sufficient inducement, surely, to the careful study of the laws governing the relation on between the individual and the Universal Mind."

To my mind, then as now, this quotation outlines the core and center of the method and manner of approach necessary for coming in touch with Infinite Supply. At least it, together with the previously quoted statement, "My mind is a center of Divine operation," etc., constituted the only apparent means of attracting to myself the twenty thousand dollars. My constant endeavor to get into the spirit of these statements, and to attract to myself this needed sum, took about six weeks, at the end of which time I had in my bank the required twenty thousand dollars. This could be made into a long story, giving all the details, but the facts, as already narrated, will give you a definite idea of the magnetic condition of my mind while the twenty thousand dollars was finding its way to me.

CHAPTER TEN

How I Became the Only Personal Pupil of T. Troward, the Great Mental Scientist

As soon as the idea of studying with Troward came to me, I asked a friend to write him for me, feeling that perhaps my friend could couch my desire in better or more persuasive terms than I could employ. To all the letters written by this friend, I received not one reply. This was so discouraging that I would have completely abandoned the idea of becoming Troward's pupil, except for the experience I had had that day on the street, when my whole world was illuminated, and

I remembered the promise "All things whatsoever thou wilt, believe thou hast received, and thou shalt receive."

With this experience in my mind, my passage to England was arranged, notwithstanding the fact that apparently my letters were ignored. We wrote again, however, and finally received a reply, very courteous though very positive. Troward did not take pupils; he had no time to devote to a pupil. Notwithstanding this definite decision, I declined to be discouraged, because of the memory of my experience upon the day when the light and the thought had come to me, "I Am all the Substance there is." I seemed to be able to live that experience over at will, and with it there always came a flood of courage and renewed energy. We journeyed on to London, and from there telegraphed Troward, asking for an interview. The telegram was promptly answered, setting a date when he could see us.

At this time Troward was living in Ruan Manor, a little out-of-the-way place in the Southern part of England, about twenty miles from a railway station. We could not find it on the map, and with great difficulty Cook's Touring Agency, in London, located the place for us. There was very little speculation in my mind as to what Troward would say to me in this interview. There always remained the feeling that the truth was mine; also that it would grow and expand in my consciousness until peace and contentment were outward, as well as inward, manifestations of my individual life.

We arrived at Troward's house in a terrific rain-storm, and were cordially received by Troward himself, whom I found, much to my surprise, to be more the type of a Frenchman than an English-man, (I afterward learned that be was a descendant of the Huguenot race), a man of medium stature, with a rather large head, big nose, and eyes that fairly danced with merriment. After we had been introduced to the other members of the family and given a cup of hot tea, we were invited into the living-room, where Troward talked very freely of everything except my proposed studies. It seemed quite impossible to bring him to that subject. Just before we were leaving, however, I asked quite boldly: "Will you not reconsider your decision to take a personal pupil? I wish so much to study with you," to which he replied, with a very indifferent manner, that he did not feel he could give the time it would require for personal instruction, but that he would be glad to give me the names of two or three books which he felt would not only be inter-esting but instructive to me. He said he felt much flattered and pleased that I had come all the way from America to study with him, and as we walked out through the lane from his house to our automobile, his manner became less indifferent, a feeling of sympathy seemed to touch his heart, and he turned to me with the remark: "You might write to me, if so inclined, after you get to Paris, and perhaps, if I have time in the autumn, we could arrange something, though it does not seem possible now."

I lost no time in following up his very kind invitation to write. My letters were all promptly and courteously answered, but there was never a word of encouragement as to my proposed studies, Finally, about two months later, there came a letter with this question in it: "What do you suppose is the meaning of this verse in the twenty-first Chapter of Revelation?"

"16. And the city lieth foursquare and the length is as large as the breadth; and he measured the city with the reed, twelve thousand furlongs. The length and the breadth and the height of it are equal."

Instinctively I knew that my chance to study with Troward hung upon my giving the correct answer to that question. The definition of the verse seemed utterly beyond my reach. Naturally, answers came to my mind, but I knew intuitively that they were incorrect. I began bombarding my scholarly friends and acquaintances with the same questions. Lawyers, doctors, priests, nuns, and clergymen, all over the world, received letters from me with this question in them. Answers began to return to me, but intuition told me not one was correct. All the while I was endeavoring to find the answer for myself, but no answer came. I memorized the verse in order that I might meditate upon it. I began a search of Paris for the books Troward had recommended to me, and after two or three days' search we crossed the River Seine to the Ile de Cite to go into some of the old bookstores there. The books were out of print, and these were the last places in which to find them. Finally we came upon a little shop which had them. The man had only one copy of each left, consequently the price was high. While remonstrating with the clerk, my eye rested upon the work of an astrologer, which I laughingly picked up and asked: "Do you think Prof.—— would read my horoscope?" The clerk looked aghast at the suggestion, and responded, "Why, no, Madame, he is one of France's greatest astrologers. He does not read horoscopes."

In spite of this answer, there was a persistent impulse within me to go to the man. The friend who had accompanied me in my search for the books remonstrated with me, and tried in every way to dissuade me from going to the famous astrologer, but I insisted. When we arrived at his office, I found it somewhat embarrassing to ask him to read my horoscope. Nevertheless, there was nothing to do but put the question. Reluctantly, the Professor invited us into his paper-strewn study; reluctantly, and also impatiently he asked us to be seated. Very courteously and coldly he told me that he did not read horoscopes. His whole manner said, more clearly than words could, that he wished we would take our departure.

My friend stood up. I was at a great loss what to do next, because I felt that I was not quite ready to go. Intuition seemed to tell me there was something for me to gain there. Just what it was I was unable to define, so I paused a moment, much to my friend's displeasure and embarrassment, when one of the Professor's enormous Persian cats jumped into my lap. "Get down, Jack!" the Professor shouted. "What does it mean?" he seemed to ask himself. Then with a greater interest than he had hitherto shown in me, the Professor said with a smile:

"I have never known that cat to go to a stranger before, Madame; my cat pleads for you. I, also, now feel an interest in your horoscope, and if you will give me the data it will give me pleasure to write it out for you."

There was a great feeling of happiness in me when he made this statement, which he concluded by saying, "I do not feel that you really care for your horoscope." The truth of this statement shocked me, because I did not care about a horoscope, and could not give any reason why I was letting him do it. "However," he said, "may I call for your data next Sunday afternoon?"

On Sunday afternoon at the appointed time, the Professor arrived, and I was handing him the slip of paper with all the data of my birth, etc., when the idea came to ask the Professor the answer to the question Troward bad given me from the 16th verse of the twenty-first Chapter of Revelation. The thought was instantly carried into effect, and I found myself asking this man what he thought this verse meant. Without pausing to think it over, he immediately replied, "It means: the city signifies the truth, and the truth is non-invertible; every side from which you approach it is exactly the same." Intuitively and undoubtingly I recognized this answer as the true one, and my joy knew no bounds, because I felt sure that with this correct answer in my possession, Troward would accept me as his pupil in the fall.

As the great astrologer was leaving, I explained to him all about my desire to study with Troward, how I had come from New York City for that express purpose, seemingly to no avail, until the answer to this test question had been given to me by him. He was greatly interested and asked many questions about Troward, and when asked if he would please send me his bill, he smilingly replied, "Let me know if the great Troward accepts you as his pupil," and bade me good afternoon. I hastened to my room to send a telegram to Troward, giving my answer to the question from the 16th verse of the 21st Chapter of Revelation.

There was an immediate response from Troward which said: "Your answer is correct. Am beginning a course of lectures on The Great Pyramid in London. If you wish to attend them, will be pleased to have you, and afterward, if you still wish to study with me, I think it can be arranged." On receipt of this reply preparations were at once made to leave Paris for London.

I attended all the lectures, receiving much instruction from them, after which arrangements were made for my studying with Troward. Two days before leaving for Cornwall, I received the following letter from Troward clearly indicating the line of study he gave me:

31 Stanwick Road,

W. Kensington, England.

Dear Mrs. Behrend:

I think I had better write you a few lines with regard to your proposed studies with me, as I should be sorry for you to be under any misapprehension and so to suffer any disappointment.

I have studied the subject now for several years, and have a general acquaintance with the leading features of most of the systems which, unfortunately, occupy attention in many circles at the present time, such as Theosophy, The Tarot, The Kabala, and the like, and I have no hesitation in saying that, to the best of my judgment, all sorts and descriptions of *so-called* occult study are in direct opposition to the real life-giving Truth, and therefore, you must not expect any teaching on such lines as these.

We hear a great deal these days about initiation; but, believe me, the more you try to become a so-called "Initiate" the further you will put yourself from living life.

I speak after many years of careful study and consideration when I say that the Bible and its Revelation of Christ is the one thing really worth studying, and that is a subject large enough in all conscience, embracing, as it does, our outward life and of everyday concerns, and also the inner springs of our life and all that we can in general terms conceive of the life in the unseen after putting off the body at death.

You have expressed a very great degree of confidence in my teaching, and if your confidence is such that you wish, as you say, to put yourself entirely under my guidance, I can only accept it as a very serious responsibility, and should have to ask you to exhibit that confidence by refusing to look into such so-called "Mysteries" as I would forbid you to look into.

I am speaking from experience; but the result will be that much of my teaching will appear to be very simple, perhaps to some extent dogmatic, and you will say you have heard much of it before.

Faith in God, Prayer and Worship, approach to the Father through Christ—all this is in a certain sense familiar to you; and all I can hope to do is perhaps to throw a little more light on these subjects, that they may become to you, not merely traditional words, but *present living facts*.

I have been thus explicit as I do not want you to have any disappointment, and also I should say that our so-called course of study will be only friendly conversations at such times as we can fit them in, either you coming to our house, or I to yours, as may be most convenient at the time.

Also, I will lend you some books which will be helpful, but they are very few, and in no sense occult.

Now, if all this falls in with your ideas, we shall, I am sure, be very glad to see you at Ruan Manor, and you will find that the residents there, though few, are very friendly and the neighborhood very pretty.

But, on the other hand, if you feel that you want some other source of learning, do not mind saying so, only you will never find any substitute for Christ.

I trust you will not mind my writing you like this, but I do not want you to come all the way down to Cornwall, and then be disappointed.

With kindest regards,
Yours sincerely,
(Signed) T. Troward.

This copy of Troward's letter, to my mind, is the greatest thing I can give you.

CHAPTER ELEVEN

How to Bring the Power in Your Word Into Action

In every word you use, there is a power germ which expands and projects itself in the direction your word indicates, and ultimately develops into physical expression. For example, you wish the consciousness of joy. Repeat the word "joy" secretly, persistently and emphatically. The repetition of the word joy sets up a quality of vibration which causes the joy germ to begin to expand and project itself until your whole being is filled with joy. This is not a mere fancy, but a truth. Once you experience this power, you will daily prove to yourself that these facts have not been fabricated to fit a theory, but the theory has been built up by careful observation of facts; Everyone knows that joy comes from within. No one can give it to you. Another may give you cause for joy, but no one can be joyous for you. Joy is a state of consciousness, and consciousness is purely mental.

Troward says the "Mental faculties always work under something which stimulates them, and this stimulus may come either from without, through the external senses, or from within, by the consciousness of something not perceptible on the physical plane. The recognition of this interior source of stimulus enables you to bring into your consciousness any state you desire." Once a thing seems normal to you, it is as surely yours, through the Law of growth and attraction, as it is yours to know addition after you have learned the use of figures.

This method of repeating the word makes the word in all of its limitless meaning yours, because words are the embodiment of thoughts, and thought is creative; neither good nor bad, simply creative. This is the reason why Faith builds up and Fear destroys.

"Only believe, and all things are possible unto you."

It is Faith that gives you dominion over every adverse circumstance or condition. It is your word of Faith that sets you free not faith in any specific thing or act, but simple Faith in your best self in all ways. It is this ever-present Creative Power within the heart of the word that makes your health, your peace of mind, and your financial condition a reproduction of your most habitual thought. Try to believe and understand this, and you will find yourself Master of every adverse circumstance or condition, for you will become a Prince of Power.

CHAPTER TWELVE

How to Increase Your Faith

But you ask, "How can I speak the word of Faith when I have little or no faith?"

Every living thing has faith in something or somebody. Faith is that quality of Power which gives the Creative Energy a corresponding vitality, and the vitality in the word of Faith you use causes it to take corresponding physical form. Even intense fear is alive with faith. You fear smallpox because you *believe* it possible for you to contract it. You fear poverty and loneliness because you *believe* them possible for you. It is the Faith which understands that every creation had its birth in the womb of thought-words, that gives you dominion over all things, your lesser self included, and this feeling of faith is increased and intensified through observing what it *does*.

Your constant observation should be of your state of consciousness when you did; not when you hoped you might, but feared it was too good to be true. How did you feel that time when you simply bad to bring yourself into a better frame of mind and did, or you had to have a certain thing and got it? Live these experiences over again and again—mentally—until you really feel in touch with the self which knows and does, and then the best there is, is yours.

CHAPTER THIRTEEN

The Reward of Increased Faith

Your desire to be your best has expanded your faith into the faith of the Universe which knows no failure, and has brought you into conscious realization that you are not a victim of the universe, but a part of it. Consequently you are able to recognize that there is that within yourself which is able to make conscious contact with the Universal Law, and enables you to press all the particular laws of Nature, whether visible or invisible, into serving your particular demand or desire. Thereby you find yourself Master, not a slave, of any situation. Troward tells us that this Mastering is to be "accomplished by knowledge, and the only knowledge which will afford this purpose in all its measureless immensity is the knowledge of the personal element in universal spirit," and its reciprocity to our own personality. In other words, the words you think, the personality you feel yourself to be, are all reproductions in miniature of God, "or specialized universal spirit." All your word-thoughts were God word-forms before they were yours.

The words you use are the instruments—channels—through which the creative energy takes form. Naturally, this sensitive Creative Power can only reproduce in accordance with the instrument through which it passes. All disappointments and failures are the result of endeavoring to think one thing and produce another. This is just as impossible as it would be for an electric fan to be used for lighting purposes, or for water to flow through a crooked pipe in a straight line. The water must take the shape of the pipe through which it flows. Even more truly this sensitive, invisible Substance must reproduce outwardly the shape of the thought-word through which it passes.

This is the law of its Nature; therefore, it logically follows,

"As a man thinketh, so is he."

Hence, when your thought or word-form is in correspondence with the Eternal constructive and forward movement of the Universal Law, then your mind is the mirror in which the Infinite Power and Intelligence of the Universe sees itself reproduced, and your individual life becomes one of harmony.

CHAPTER FOURTEEN

How to Make Nature Respond to You

It should be steadily borne in mind that there is an Intelligence and Power in all Nature and all space, which is always creative, and infinitely sensitive and responsive. The responsiveness of its nature is two-fold: it is creative, and amenable to suggestion. Once the human understanding grasps this all-important fact, it realizes the simplicity with which the law of life supplies your every demand. All that is necessary is to realize that your mind is a center of Divine operation, and consequently contains that within itself which accepts suggestions, and expect all life to respond to your call.

Then you will find suggestions which tend to the fulfillment of your desire coming to you, not only from your fellowmen, but also from the flowers, the grass, the trees, and the rocks, which will enable you to fulfill your heart's desire, if you act upon them in confidence on this physical plane. "Faith without works is dead," but Faith *with* Works sets you absolutely free.

CHAPTER FIFTEEN

Faith With Works— What It Has Accomplished

It is said of Tyson, the great Australian Million-aire, that the suggestion to "make the desert land of Australia blossom as the rose" came to him from a modest little Australian violet while he was working as a bushman for something like three shillings a day. He used to find these friendly little violets growing in certain places in the woods, and something in the flower touched something akin to itself in the mind of Tyson. He would sit on the side of his bunk at night and wonder how

flowers and vegetable life could be given an oppor-
tunity to express themselves in the desert land of
Australia. No doubt he realized that it would take
a long time to save enough money to put irrigat-
ing ditches in the desert lands, but his thought and
feeling assured him it could be accomplished, and
if it could be done, he could do it. If there was a
power within himself which was able to capture
the idea, then there must be a responsive power
within the idea itself which could bring itself into
a practical physical manifestation. He resolutely
put aside all questions as to the specific ways and
means which would be employed in bringing his
desire into physical manifestation, and simply
kept his thought centered upon the idea of making fences and seeing flowers and grass where none
existed at that time.

Since the responsiveness of Reproductive Creative Power is not limited to any local condition
of mind, his habitual meditation and mental picture set his ideas free to roam in an infinitude,
and attract to themselves other ideas of a kindred
nature.

Therefore, it was not necessary for Tyson to
wait until he bad saved from his three shillings a
day enough money to irrigate the land, to see his
ideas and desires fulfilled, for his ideas found other
ideas in the financial world which were attuned in

sympathy with themselves, and doors of finance were quickly opened.

All charitable institutions are maintained upon the principle of the responsiveness of life. If this were not true, no one would care to give, simply because another needed.

The law of demand and supply, cause and effect, can never be broken. Ideas attract to themselves kindred ideas. Sometimes they come from a flower, a book, or out of the invisible.

You are intent upon an idea not quite complete as to the ways and means of fulfillment, and behold along comes another idea, from no one can tell where, and finds friendly lodging with your idea; one idea attracting another, and so on until your desires are physical facts. You may feel the necessity for improvement in your finances, and wonder how this increase is to be brought about, when there seems suddenly to come from within the idea itself, the realization that everything—even money—had its birth in thought, and your thoughts turn their course. You simply hold to the statement or affirmation that the best, and all there is, is yours. Since you are able to capture ideas from the Infinite through the instrument of your intuition, you let your mind rest upon that thought, knowing full well that this very thought will respond to itself. Your inhibition of all doubt and anxiety enables the reassuring ideas to establish themselves and attract to themselves "I can" and "I will" ideas, which gradually grow into the physical form of the desire in your mind.

In the conscious uses of the Universal Power to reproduce your desires in physical form, three facts should be borne in mind:

First—All space is filled with a Creative Power.

Second—This Creative Power is amenable to suggestion.

Third—It can only work by deductive methods.

As Troward tells us, this last is an exceedingly important point, for it implies that the action of the ever-present Creative Power is in no way limited by precedent. It works according to the essence of the spirit of the principle. In other words, this Universal Power takes its creative direction from the word you give it. Once man realizes this great truth, the character with which this sensitive, reproductive power is invested becomes the most important of all his considerations. It is the unvarying law of Creative Life Principle that "As a man thinketh in his heart, so is he." If you realize the truth that the Creative Power can be to you only what you feel and think it to be, it is willing and able to meet your demands.

Troward says, "If you think your thought is Powerful, your Thought is Powerful."

"As a man thinketh in his heart, so is he" is the law of life, and the Creative Power can no more change this law than an ordinary mirror can reflect back to you a different image than the object you hold before it. "As you think, so are you" does not mean "as you tell people you think," or "as you would wish the world to believe you think." It means your innermost thoughts; that place where no one but you knows. "None can know the Father save the son," and "No one can know the son but the Father." Only the reproductive Creative Spirit of Life knows what you think until your thoughts become physical facts and manifest themselves in your body, your brain, or your affairs. Then everyone with whom you come into contact may know, because the Father, the Intelligent Creative Energy which heareth in secret your most secret thoughts, rewards you openly reproduces your thoughts in physical form. "As you think, that is what you become" should be kept in the background of your mind constantly. This is watching and praying without ceasing, and when you are not feeling quite up to par physically, pray.

CHAPTER
SIXTEEN

Suggestions As to How to Pray or Ask, Believing You Have Already Received

Scientific Thinking—Positive Thought Suggestions for Practical Application

Try, through careful, positive, enthusiastic (though not strenuous) thought, to realize that the indescribable, Invisible Substance of Life fills all space; that its nature is Intelligent, Undifferentiated Substance.

Five o'clock in the morning is the best time to go into this sort of meditation.

If you will retire early every night for one month, and before falling asleep, impress firmly upon your subjective mind the affirmation: "My Father is the ruler of all the world, and is expressing His directing power through me," you will find that the substance of life takes form in your thought molds. Do not accept the above suggestion simply because it is given to you. Think it over carefully until the impression is made upon your own subconscious mind understandingly. Rise every morning, as was suggested before, at five o'clock, sit in a quiet room in a straight-back chair, and think out the affirmation of the previous evening, and you will realize and be able to put into practice your Princely Power with the realization to some extent, at least, that your mind really is a center through which all the Creative Energy and Power there is, is taking form.

Scientific Prayer
The Principle Underlying Scientific Prayer

In prayer for a change in condition, physical, mental, or financial, for yourself or another, bear in mind that the fundamental necessity for the answer to prayer is the understanding of the scientific statement:

"Ask, believing you have already received, *And you shall receive*"

This is not as difficult as it appears on the surface, once you realize that:

Everything has, its origin in the mind, and that which you seek outwardly, you already possess.

No one can think a thought in the future.

Your thought of a thing constitutes its origin.

THEREFORE:

The Thought Form of the Thing
is Already Yours As soon as you think it.

Your steady recognition of this Thought Possession causes the thought to concentrate, to condense, to project itself, and to assume physical form.

To Get Rich Through Creation

The recognition or conception of new sources of wealth is the loftiest aspiration you can take into your heart, for it assumes and implies the furtherance of all noble aims.

Items to be remembered about
Prayer for Yourself or Another

Remember that that which you call treatment or prayer is not, in any sense, hypnotism. It should never be your endeavor to take possession of the mind of another.

Remember that it should never be your intention to make yourself believe that which you know to be untrue. You are simply thinking into God or First Cause with the understanding that:

"If a thing is true at all, there is a way in which it is true throughout the universe."

Remember that the power of thought works by absolutely scientific principles. These principles are expressed in the language of the statement:

"As a man thinketh in his heart, so is he." This statement contains a world of wisdom, but man's steady recognition and careful application of the statement itself is required to bring it into practical use.

Remember that the principles involved in being as we think in our heart are elucidated and revealed by the law: "As you sow, so shall you reap."

Remember that your freedom to choose just what you will think, just what thought possession you will affirm and claim, constitutes God's gift to you.

It shows how First Cause has endowed every man with the power and ability to bring into his personal environment whatever he chooses.

Cause and Effect in reference to Getting.

If you plant an ACORN, you get an OAK.

If you sow a GRAIN OF CORN, you reap a stalk and MANY kernels of corn.

You always get the manifestation of that which you consciously or unconsciously AFFIRM and CLAIM, habitually declare and expect, or, in other words, "AS YOU SOW."

Therefore, sow the seeds of—I AM . . . I OUGHT TO DO . . . I CAN DO . . . I WILL DO.

Realize
—that because you ARE you OUGHT to do;
—that because you OUGHT to, you CAN do;
—that because you CAN do, you DO do.

The manifestation of this truth, even in a small degree, gives you the undisputable understanding that DOMINION IS YOUR CHARTER RIGHT.

You are an heir of First Cause, endowed with all the power He has.

God has given you everything. ALL is yours, and you know that all you have to do is to reach out your mental hand and take it.

This Formula may serve as a pattern to shape your own Prayer or Affirmation into God for the benefit of another or yourself.

If for another, you speak the Christian name of the person you wish to help; then dismiss their personality entirely from your consciousness.

Intensify your thought by meditating upon the fact that there is that in you which finds the way, which is the Truth and is the Life.

You are affirming this fact, believing that since you are thinking this, it is already yours. Having lifted up your feeling to the central idea of this meditation, you examine your own conscious-ness and see if there is aught which is unlike God. If there is any feeling of fear, worry, malice, envy, hatred, or jealousy turn back in your meditation to cleanse your thought through the affirmation that God's love and purity fills all space, including your heart and soul. Reconcile your thought with the love of God, always remembering that:

You are made in the Image and Likeness of Love.

Keep this cleansing thought in mind until you feel that you have freed your consciousness entirely of all thoughts and feelings other than:

Love and Unity with all Humanity.

Then if denials do not disturb you, deny all that is unlike your desired manifestation. This accom-plished, you almost overlay your denial with the affirmative thought that You are made in the Image and Likeness of God, and already have your desire fulfilled in its first, its original thought-form.

Closing of prayer

Prayer as a method of thought is a deliberate use of the Law which gives you the power of dominion over everything which tends in any way to hamper your perfect liberty.

YOU HAVE BEEN GIVEN LIFE THAT YOU MAY ENJOY IT MORE AND MORE FULLY.

The steady recognition of this Truth makes you declare yourself a

PRINCE OF POWER.

You recognize, accept, and use this power as

THE CHILD OF A KING, AND HENCE DOMINION IS YOUR BIRTHRIGHT.

Then when you feel the light of this great truth flooding your consciousness—open the flood-gates of your soul in heartfelt praise because you have the understanding that

THE CREATOR AND HIS CREATION ARE ONE;

also that the Creator is continually creating through his creation.

Close your treatment in the happy assurance that the prayer which is fulfilled is not a form of supplication, but a steady habitual affirming that: "The Creator of all creation is operating specifically through me," therefore—

THE WORK MUST BE PERFECTLY DONE.
YOUR MIND IS A CENTER
OF DIVINE OPERATION

Hints for application and Practice

For every five minutes given to reading and study of the theories of Mental Science, spend fifteen minutes in the use and application of the knowledge acquired.

1. Spend one minute in every twenty-four hours to conscientiously thinking over the specification that must be observed in order to have your prayers answered.

2. Practice the steady recognition of desirable thought possession for two periods of fifteen minutes each every day. Not only time yourself each

period to see how long you can keep a given conception before your mental vision, but also keep a written record of the vividness with which you experience your mental image. Remember that your mental senses are just as varied and trainable as your physical ones.

3. Spend five minutes every day between 12 noon and 1 o'clock with a mental research for new sources of wealth.

CHAPTER SEVENTEEN

Things to Remember

That the greatest Mental Scientist the world has ever known (Jesus Christ, the Man) said all things are possible unto you. Also, "the things I do, you can do." Did he tell the truth?

Jesus did not claim to be more divine than you are. He declared the whole human race children of God. By birth he was no exception to this rule. The power be possessed was developed through His personal effort. He said you could do the same if you would only believe in yourself.

A great idea is valueless unless accompanied by physical action. God gives the idea; man works it out upon the physical plane.

All that is really worth while is contentment. Self-command alone can produce it.

The soul and body are one. Contentment of mind is contentment of soul, and contentment of soul means contentment of body.

If you wish health, watch your thoughts, not only of your physical being, but your thoughts about everything and everybody. With your will, keep them in line with your desire, and outwardly act in accordance with your thoughts, and you will soon realize that all power both over thoughts and conditions has been given to you.

You believe in God. Believe in yourself as the physical instrument through which God operates.

Absolute dominion is yours when you have sufficient self-mastery to conquer the negative tendency of thoughts and actions.

Ask yourself daily: "What is the purpose of the Power which put me here?"

"How can I work with the purpose for life and liberty in me?"

After having decided these questions, endeavor hourly to fulfill them. You are a law unto yourself.

If you have a tendency to overdo *anything*: eat, drink, or blame circumstances for your misfortunes, conquer that tendency with the inward conviction that *all power* is yours. Eat less, drink less, blame circumstances less, and the best there is will gradually grow in the place where the worst seemed to be.

Always remember that all is yours to use as you will. You can if you *will*; if you *will*, you do.

God the Father blesses you with all He has to give. Make good Godly use of it.

The reason for greater success when you first began your studies and demonstrations in Mental Science, was your joy and enthusiasm at the simple discovery of Power within, which was greater than you were able to put into your understanding later. With increased understanding comes increasing joy and enthusiasm, and the results will correspond.

ABOUT THE AUTHOR

Genevieve Behrend (1881 in Paris–1960 in United States) was a French-born author and teacher of Mental Science, a New Thought discipline created by Thomas Troward.

There is little known about her early life except that one of her parents was Scottish. After her husband died she traveled extensively. She studied Christian Science and met its founder Mary Baker Eddy, but ultimately left that faith. She met Abdul Baha, whose father had founded Bahá'í Faith, and he told her that she would "travel the world over seeking the truth, and when [she] had found it, would speak it out." She later wrote that she found a book of Thomas Troward's lectures. Inspired by this, she wanted to study with Troward (who was known as the master of Mental Science), but lacked the money to travel to Cornwall, England where he lived, as she was then living in New York. So every night and morning she visualized counting out twenty $1,000 bills, buying her ticket to London, traveling on the ship, and being accepted as Troward's pupil. She also constantly affirmed to herself, "My mind is a center of Divine operations." Then, to quote her in *Your Invisible Power*:

> "While these reflections were going on in my mind, there seemed to come up from within me the thought: 'I am all the substance there is.' Then, from another channel in my brain the answer seemed to come, 'Of course, that's it; everything must have its beginning in mind. The 'I', the Idea, must be the only one and primary substance there is, and this means money as well as everything else.' My mind accepted this idea, and immediately all the tension of mind and body was relaxed."

In about six weeks, she received the money. From 1912 to 1914, her life focused solely on the wisdom and philosophy of Troward whose influential and compelling ideas provided much of the groundwork to the spiritual philosophy known today as New Thought. As the awareness of "mental science" was taking shape, Troward imparted his personal insight to only one pupil who could perpetuate this knowledge and share it with the world. Behrend was the only personal student Troward had throughout his life.

After her studies with Troward, around 1915, she founded a New Thought school called The School of the Builders in New York City, running it herself until 1925. She then established another school in Los Angeles before touring other major cities throughout North America for the next 35 years as a celebrated lecturer, teacher, and practitioner of "Mental Science." She is quoted as an expert in the best-selling self-help book *The Secret* by Rhonda Byrne.

Millions heard and enjoyed her, not only on the public platform but over the radio. Her students numbered tens of thousands all over the English-speaking world. *Your Invisible Power* was her first book and remains her most powerful and popular work, and, since its first edition, one of the world's best sellers on Mental Science. It has exhausted scores of editions.

Behrend presents the Troward philosophy at its best because of the way her incomparably direct, and dynamic personality relates the life-changing concepts on a personal level.

This book can teach you how to use the power of visualization and other processes taught by Thomas Troward to transform your life. *Your Invisible Power* is a powerful, yet simple and easy guide.

Behrend says, "We all possess more power and greater possibilities than we realize, and visualizing is one of the greatest of these powers. It brings other possibilities to our observation. When we pause to think for a moment, we realize that for a cosmos to exist at all, it must be the outcome of a cosmic mind. These pages have been written with the purpose and hope that their suggestions may furnish you a key to open up the way to the attainment of your desires."

This book can teach you how to use the power of visualization and other processes taught by Thomas Troward to transform your life.